YOUNG ALEXANDRA

The Early Life of Alexandra Teploff née Meyendorff

EION MCRAE

ISBN 978-1-54397642-7 (print)
ISBN 978-1-54397-643-4 (eBook)

CONTENTS

SCRIBE'S FOREWORD

"**Y**ou should call Alexandra Teploff." That's what people told me.

My wife, Jean, and I, recently retired, had moved into our new home in Tewksbury Township in Hunterdon County, New Jersey, and we were dreaming of vacations in France—especially in Deep France, where talking Anglo gets you nowhere. I needed to brush up my French with a tutor.

So I called Alexandra Teploff, and immediately found myself engrossed in a pleasant chat, in French, about our respective family backgrounds. I learned that she was born in St Petersburg, Russia, ten years before the 1917 revolution. This meant she was in her mid-eighties, which I found hard to credit since her voice had the vibrant tone of a much younger woman's. Later, from other Tewksbury residents I learned that Alexandra had been a beloved teacher and a power in local arts and theater for almost fifty years, and showed little sign of slowing down. Everyone I talked to mentioned the great enthusiasm she brought to every activity, from playing tennis to playing various musical instruments from flute to percussion. As a tennis player she was known for her extreme enthusiasm for the sport. After being sidelined by an injury to her right shoulder, she made a long, totally unsuccessful attempt to come back as a leftie. As a music student she was known for making a thunderous racket on drums.

1

Alexandra spoke fluent French with an accent—a Swiss accent I learned later—that is easier for English-speakers to understand than Parisian. And yes, *bien sûr,* she was ready to help me. All I had to do was come upstairs at the local library, the Tewksbury Township Library in Oldwick, for a French-oriented get-together on Wednesday mornings at ten.

Those weekly meetings were relaxed affairs, maybe five or six attendees spanning the gamut of language ability, attempting to converse in French. There was no charge or obligation, no formal agenda, no textbook, very little actual teaching—but a great deal of good-natured laughter, for Alexandra's joy in speaking French was infectious.

As a rule she set the conversation rolling with some prepared topic, and kept a few fresh topics ready for those moments when the conversation became irretrievably tangled. She answered questions at the level of proficiency of the person who asked them, and she tactfully corrected extremely un-French locutions, like the *mon femme* sort of thing. (It should be *ma femme,* since *femme,* meaning wife in this case, is a feminine noun.) Aside from that she simply let people carry on as they pleased, even if they did so in English.

While Alexandra's *réunions* were a pleasant way for people to brush up their French skills, for beginners they weren't very efficient; they lacked the frequent reinforcement needed to ensure that a word or phrase picked up at one session will be recalled at the next. But nobody came with learning the language at the top of their agenda. Mainly, I think, they came out of personal regard for Alexandra, the recognition that here was a person profoundly happy, one who had mastered the art of living.

What does it mean to master the art of living? Of course nobody can say for sure, but few doubt that developing a kindly and generous sense of humor is part of it. It was Alexandra's disposition to smile, often to laugh, at anything quaintly out of kilter, particularly the unintentional mangling of meaning that sometimes accompanies translation from one language to another. Here's an example of the sort of joke she told from time to time, always with a laugh. Sign in a swanky Zurich hotel: "Guests are respectfully reminded that it is contrary to hotel policy to entertain persons of the opposite sex in the rooms. Those activities should be pursued in the lobby."

It wasn't necessary for a joke to be clever. Alexandra valued wit, however modest, as long as it was charitable. She drew the line at the unkind or derisive, and showed her disapproval by feigning deafness.

The sudden-deaf conversation stopper is disconcerting to us Anglo speakers, but it is okay in a French context. It serves a purpose. If talk turns embarrassing, it makes sense to cut it.

Alexandra gave me a particularly educational silent treatment in the course of one of what I call our "laugh-ins." Between us we recalled most of the venerable cartoon collection "Fractured French," by F S Pearson and R Taylor, and we were laughing ourselves silly swapping its zany mistranslations. I recalled the cartoon of a woman who'd grossly over imbibed at a cocktail party, captioned *Carte blanche* "For God's sake, take Blanche home," and we both laughed. But when I mentioned the cartoon depicting a gaggle of painted woman marching in a vaguely military setting, captioned *Hors de combat* "Camp followers," I laughed alone. I thought at first that Alexandra had not heard the joke, and—I hate to admit this—I repeated it. Only then did I realize I was getting the sudden-deaf signal to shut up. While Alexandra was open to jokes about human failings like occasional drunkenness, she saw prostitution as a great evil and certainly no laughing manner. As a rule, though, laughter came to her as naturally as breathing.

Also natural to her was the love of music, and she longed to engage others in it. To that end, before I came on the scene, she had organized what became known as the Living-room Concert Series. She had tapped numerous friends who happened to have large living rooms with good acoustics and, preferably, a Steinway; and other friends, also numerous, who happened to be excellent musicians, to perform classical chamber music in conditions like those envisaged by the composers.

What a wonderful idea! Unfortunately, like many a wonderful idea, it bloomed, then fizzled—in this case, for lack of an audience. In the beginning, Alexandra had found more than enough listeners to fill a living room, but most of them came to please her, not for music.

Alexandra was slow to accept the reality there are many perfectly nice people who are not thrilled by chamber music, and she longed to revive her beautiful idea. Jean and I tried to help by rationalizing and expanding Alexandra's mailing list (she had never heard of computers), and helping round up musicians. We put on three concerts that were respectable with regard to performance, and one that was outstanding—a piano recital by three fine artists and academics, long-time friends of Alexandra's. But the turnout was sparse, and reluctantly, she gave up.

The average attendance at Alexandra's reunions also gradually declined as people moved away and fewer came to replace them, so it occasionally happened that I was the sole attendee. Alexandra did not seem to mind this in the least. "Now we'll have a really good chat," she said. And so we did, often nattering away in French—fractured French on my part—for a couple of hours with hardly a pause.

We never had to struggle to find a topic of mutual interest. Alexandra drew on a deeply ingrained appreciation of Russian and French literature. She talked about the characters created by Tolstoy and Balzac, including her favorite literary persona, Prince Andrei in *War and Peace*, as if they were actual people she just happened to be acquainted with. She had the wit and easy confidence to engage in topics she initially knew next to nothing about. I recall our having a "really good chat" about Darwin's theory of evolution and its extension at the molecular (DNA) level.

Alexandra in 2004, age 97.

But what I found most fascinating in my one-on-one meetings with Alexandra were her recollections of her childhood in Russia in the turmoil of the 1910s, her coming of age in Estonia, and youth in England and America. She was not especially keen on talking about herself and her experiences; she was more apt to inquire how *you* feel and what *you* think about things. So her personal story came out in disconnected fragments. Little by little, however, and with Alexandra's help, I pieced it together and set it down here.

I completed a draft in 2004, and Alexandra approved eventual publication. She permitted me to make use of family photos and of a set of pastel drawings illustrating her life in the time of the Russian Revolution. I made copies and returned the originals to her.

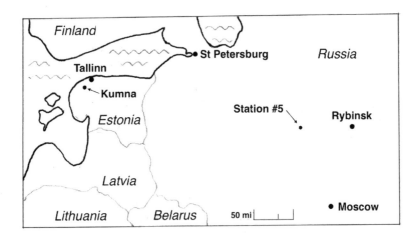

In addition to the above map, I append for reference a timeline of Alexandra's youth in relation to world events.

Now, dear readers, with those preliminaries out of the way, I wish you what Alexandra would have called "a really good read."

1

St Petersburg and Kumna

Alexandra Teploff, née Meyendorff, was born in St Petersburg, Russia, in 1907. It was a time of gathering political foment foreshadowing the outbreak of the Russian Revolution of 1917.

The name Meyendorff was already well known in the Middle Ages. Its most celebrated bearer served as Bishop of Bamberg, as Chancellor to the German King Henry III, and ultimately as Pope Clement II, before he died only ten months into his reign—assassinated by poisoning, according to family lore—in 1047. By the beginning of the 20th century, closely related branches of the family had prospered in Eastern Europe for several generations. Between them they owned vast tracts of farmland and forest in German-speaking Estonia and Latvia, as well as in the Ukraine area of Southwest Russia.

Alexandra's grandfathers were brothers, Théodore and Théophile Meyendorff. (Their use of French given names reflects the preference among the Russian aristocracy for the French language over their native Russian or German. They occasionally went by native-language names, Théodore by the German, Fritz, and Théophile by the Russian, Feofil.)

Both grandfathers were career cavalry officers and landholders, but by the turn of the century their ways had parted.

Théodore Meyendorff

Théodore, Alexandra's paternal grandfather, retired to his rural estate in Ukraine, and rarely saw other branches of the family. Alexandra remembered him for allowing her and her younger sister, Maya, to sit on his knees and tug the twin forks of his beard.

Meanwhile, Théophile rose in the military ranks and eventually commanded the Russian forces in the Russo-Japanese War of

1905. His civilian career was no less distinguished; he served in St Petersburg as a confidential aide, first to Tsar Alexander III and then to his successor, Nicholas II. In another important role, Théodore reveled in the theatrical trappings of war, beautiful horses and smart uniforms. Himself a dashing figure astride a white charger, he took pride in overseeing ceremonial parades on the esplanade opposite the Winter Palace in St Petersburg.

Théophile Meyendorff

Alexandra's father, Vasily, was the son of Théodore and his wife Marsha, and heir, jointly with a sister, to his parents' country estate in Ukraine. In youth, Vasily learned something of the business of farming, and he enjoyed rural diversions like horseback riding and hunting. He also had a zest for the technology of the period, and he dreamed of a career as an engineer.

At the time, Russia was straining to catch up with the nineteenth-century advances in rail transportation that had already led to great economic benefits in Britain and Western Europe. A functioning national rail system was urgently needed to tap into the country's heartland, as well as for strategic advantage in a long-simmering dispute—eventually, in 1905, war—with Japan.

Probably for that reason, Vasily's inclination to engineering won out over the prospect of managing the Ukraine estate. He studied civil engineering at St Petersburg Polytechnic Institute, and upon graduation he obtained a position as a planning engineer in the national rail system.

In person, Vasily became a citified young man with an eye for feminine elegance—a dandy who stepped neatly in the mazurka and had a weakness for wearing costume hats. Still, he retained a residue of his early enthusiasm for farming and working with farm animals.

Alexandra's maternal grand mother, Hélène Meyendorff née Countess Schouwaloff, was a woman of intellect, artistic talent and zest for life, and she ultimately came to play a key role in Alexandra's young life.

Théophile and Hélène lived in a three-story brownstone townhouse located at 10 Pervaya Linia, Vasilevskiya Island in St Petersburg. Their children—thirteen of them!—were born and brought up there. One of the thirteen was Sofia Meyendorff, Alexandra's mother.

Hélène Meyendorff

(The street name Pervaya Linia, meaning First Line, comes from the survey line to mark the first of several boat channels across the island that were part of Peter the Great's original plan for the city, but never excavated.)

After their marriage, Vasily and Sofia took one floor of 10 Pervaya Linia as their principal home. Alexandra was born there in 1907, and her sister Marie, usually called Maya, two years later.

Number 10 Pervaya Linia

Though not nearly so imposing as many other residences in the city, 10 Pervaya Linia served as background to a domestic lifestyle of complexity and opulence difficult for us to imagine nowadays. The depth of a city block—from First Line to Second Line—the house required for its functioning numerous servants including a chef, a butler, a seamstress to sew and maintain the ladies' gowns, sundry maids and footmen, nurses to care for the younger children, and governesses and teachers for the older ones' schooling.

There were also a number of personal attendants for different family members. Théophile had two menservants, and their personalities and relationship to their employer throw light on Alexandra's life as a young child.

The senior servant, a man of about Théophile's age who had been working for him for many years, took responsibility for his employer's most important accouterments, such as his linens and dress uniforms. Somewhat stout, deliberate in manner and impeccably dignified, this man conveyed to five-year-old Alexandra an air of infallibility that placed him on a plane only slightly below that of the deity. The other manservant was a personable young man, an orphan, whom Théophile had plucked out of a life of squalor, educated and installed as a servant in his own household. The protégé's gratitude and his mastery of his duties as a valet were of great satisfaction to Théophile.

All the children were educated at home, and one subject, French, was compulsory from the start. Fluency in that language was needed to function in society; people customarily switched back and forth between Russian and French, depending on the particular thought they wished to express, and French was always used in conversation when servants were present. For that reason every household with children required at least one French governess.

The St Petersburg branch of the Myendorff family also owned a country estate known as Kumna, in Estonia. It is located near the small town of Keila, about 20 miles south-west of the capital, Kallinn, and about 250 miles from St Petersburg. Every summer for many years the family moved there, with most of their servants, for a two-month vacation.

The estate was established in the early nineteenth century by Alexandra's great-grandfather Friedrich Meyendorff. It consisted mainly of rich agricultural land, enough to support about a hundred peasant families—serfs, in Friedrich's day. It also included a large residential area with a pond and magnificent ornamental trees such as oak, fir, and a tree similar to the North-American maple that was likewise valued for its sap. In that park-like setting stood a two-story timber house with ample space for the St Petersburg Meyendorffs and their guests and entourage. Recently restored, it nowadays serves as a conference center.

Near this main house stood a smaller one in the style of a Swiss chalet with a balcony all around. It was owned by a relative, known to Alexandra as "Uncle Golitskin," who opted to spend his summers with his St Petersburg kinfolk. There were also stables, a blacksmith shop, and cottages for the estate's maintenance workers.

Alexandra's impressions of the family's arrivals at Keila are a delicious meld of fact and family legend: sun shining on a fresh spring day, peasants crowding the little train station to greet the owners with smiles and exclamations over the growth of children and grandchildren, the new babies in their nurses' arms ... and so on in the same vein.

From this account it might seem that members of the Meyendorff and other aristocratic families lived an easy life, but that was not the case. Certainly they were free from the unrelenting drudgery that was the lot of most people of the period. But the majority of the aristocracy held themselves to high standards of education and decorum. They accepted responsibilities, some of them no doubt irksome. And on the whole they strove to do their duty, as they saw it, to promote the well-being of their families and of Russian society as a whole. There were some who abused their privileges, lived for pleasure and vied to outdo each other in lavish balls and spectacles, but the Meyendorffs distanced themselves from such excesses.

Alexandra's early childhood was like a succession of storybook images and events in old St Petersburg—pretty dresses, parties, dancing lessons, military parades. The family held private celebrations for Christmas and Easter and lesser church festivals, and for the name days of family members. Because of her respected position as matriarch, Grandmother Hélène had an especially festive name day.

Those events were sometimes held at the home of Alexandra's favorite aunt, "Aunt Lily" as Alexandra called her, her mother's sister Countess Hélène (Lily) Sheremetiev. The Sheremetievs resided in a splendid mansion in the center of the old city, south of the Neva. A place of imposing columns, glittering chandeliers and elegant high-ceilinged salons, the mansion occasionally served as the venue for the most select social events in St Petersburg. But Aunt Lily, like her parents and other members of the Meyendorff family, did not much care for grand formal affairs; family gatherings were more to her taste.

Alexandra took dancing lessons starting at age five. The lessons were conducted by a dance master for the children of four or five families, and they were held in Aunt Lily's mansion—specifically at one end of the *zala*, a long hall that served in the grand houses of St Petersburg as a gallery to display portraits of the owner's august ancestors. The youngsters learned polkas and waltzes, and for a vigorous conclusion of each session, the *galop*. Alexandra adored the *galop*, especially when she had as partner her cousin Piotr, Aunt Lily's eldest son. The pair turned the dance into a boisterous game whose object was to run and slide, over the master's chiding, the entire length of the *zala*.

Most exciting of all for Alexandra was to ride in the Tsar's own carriage, a large, comfortable conveyance driven by a coachman in a crisp blue uniform, or on Sundays, a red one with gold buttons. The monarch frequently gave the vehicle to Grandfather Théophile to use on official business in St Petersburg, and from time to time Grandmother Hélène accompanied him on his rounds, along with one or two of her grandchildren. Hélène turned these excursions into mind-expanding experiences for the children, with stories, pictures and sometimes drawing lessons.

From the start, Alexandra had a happy childhood.

2

Rybinsk

Following the German onslaught on Russia after the outbreak of World War I, Vasily's work with the national railroads called him away from St Petersburg for long periods. He spent several months in the war zone, working on the repair of railroads and equipment, while Sofia and the girls remained at home at 10 Pervaya Linia. He was then reassigned to the Caucasus, in Southern Russia, where he worked on planning the rail track and the many railroad tunnels and bridges required in that mountainous area. Sofia and the two girls joined him there, and they lived for a year near the town of Sochi, on the Black Sea coast. After that the family moved north to Rybinsk, a town located some 300 miles north of Moscow.

When Alexandra turned six, her parents hired a French-speaking Swiss governess to supervise her schooling, and at the same time lay the foundation for the mastery of the French language that was necessary for an aristocratic young lady to function in society. Alexandra admired this young woman, "Mademoiselle" as she called her, feeling she must have been very brave to venture from orderly Switzerland to the wilds of the Caucasus. With Mademoiselle's help, Alexandra picked up French rapidly, and she loved the new "grown-up" language. She even begged that her arithmetic lessons be conducted in French.

With the unrest foreshadowing the Russian Revolution, and military defeats inflicted on Russia by the Germans in 1914 and 1915, the nation's fortunes went into a steep decline. Within a few years its currency collapsed and its social institutions crumbled catastrophically. Among those institutions was the privileged status of the old aristocracy.

At the beginning of this period, Vasily and his colleagues were overseeing the construction of a rail line extending westward from Rybinsk, and intended to link up with an existing north-south line to St Petersburg. Part of the track had been laid, and five of the fifteen stations planned for the completed section of the line were being built.

Vasily's particular responsibility was the track between stations numbered 4 and 5, counting from Rybinsk. This section of track and both stations were located in rural farmland. Station Number 5 was about ten miles from the nearest village, but there were hamlets within easy walking distance.

For the Meyendorff family in Rybinsk, the first signs of impending trouble were occasional shortages of funds for the railroad project. In time the shortfalls deepened, the work slowed accordingly, and Vasily often worked multiple pay periods without compensation. Eventually the government announced that it was unable to cover the engineers' salaries, and in lieu of pay it offered a one-time deed of property along the right-of-way. Vasily accepted a grant of buildings making up Station Number 5, together with several acres of the surrounding farmland.

At that point Vasily and Sofia could have opted to move away altogether, perhaps to Estonia on or near their family's estate, Kumna, or to the estate in Ukraine to which Vasily was co-heir. However, those possibilities had serious disadvantages for them. At this time Estonia wasn't quite a safe haven; towards the end of World War I the Germans had already withdrawn, but fighting was still going on between Estonian troops and Bolshevik forces. As for the properties in the Ukraine, they knew that if Vasily were to take charge of an estate there, in this time of turmoil he would automatically become a prominent person in the area, and likely a target of violence. Indeed, a few years later, three of Vasily's kinsmen in just that social position were ambushed and murdered by Bolshevik thugs. In any case the Meyendorffs felt a strong attachment to their native land, and couldn't bear the thought of fleeing to Estonia while there was still a chance that the political outlook in Russia might improve.

For those reasons the Meyendorffs elected to continue living in the Rybinsk area. For a while they remained in their home in the town, but with the increasing danger of Bolshevik violence there—and not only in Rybinsk but in towns throughout Russia—they decided to move to their property at Station Number 5 and live there, inconspicuously, as simple farmers.

Critical to the success of the plan to convert Station Number 5 to a family farm, the line from Rybinsk had been completed, ready for use, before the work came to a complete halt. This meant that livestock and supplies could be transported to the site by rail. It also meant that if the worst came to the worst and the family had to flee Russia, they would be able to do so by rail via Rybinsk. Ultimately the truncated line—the "Railroad to Nowhere," as they dubbed it—came to serve both purposes.

Brought up on a rural estate, Vasily was no stranger to farm life. He made friends with farmers and listened to their advice. Optimistic by nature, he saw his experience in the underfunded and now totally disorganized railroad system as another plus; at least he was used to things not going according to plan.

A difficulty that beset the family in their reduced circumstances was that of educating the girls, particularly eight-year-old Alexandra. They could no longer afford the services of the governess, who in any case wished case to return to Switzerland to escape the turmoil in Russia, and Sofia did not permit the girls to go to school in Rybinsk for fear of the infectious diseases rampant there.

Alexandra sorely missed her daily lessons with her kindly "Mademoiselle." However, the loss was made easier through a serendipitous discovery in an abandoned hamlet—a school library containing a trove of French-language children's books. As the walls were painted pink, they called it *"La Bibliothèque Rose"* (The Pink Library). In the solitude of that place, Alexandra, already fluent in spoken French, acquired a good reading knowledge as well.

While the move to Station Number 5 was still in the planning stage, civil institutions in Rybinsk broke down more and more quickly, and Vasily and Sofia sent the girls to live with their grandparents in the relative security of their home in St Petersburg. This was the occasion for Grandmother Hélène's most decisive influence on the two girls. With what Alexandra remembered as tremendous verve, Hélène transmitted to the girls her passion for art and literature and for life itself.

One of Hélène's lessons made a particularly lasting impression on Alexandra. Fluent in English as well as in French, Hélène enjoyed the historical romances of Sir Walter Scott, and it was through her retelling of his historical novel "Quentin Durward" that Alexandra conceived a life-long admiration of the French King Louis XI. Short of funds and of unprepossessing appearance, this fifteenth-century monarch succeeded in uniting France, with a minimum of bloodshed, despite the resistance of the bellicose Charles, Duke of Burgundy. As portrayed by Scott with his characteristically careful attention to historical accuracy, Louis XI is one of the most constructive figures in European history, emblematic of the superiority of shrewd, patient diplomacy over military might.

Once Vasily and Sofia had established their home in the bucolic safety of Station Number 5, Sofia had Alexandra and Maya sent from St Petersburg to join them, and the family set about adapting to a life very different from the one they had been brought up to.

3

Station Number 5

The Meyendorffs took over as their residence the greater part of the one substantial building at Station Number 5, allowing strangers to occupy the remaining space. They converted two railroad storage buildings to house the farm animals—a cow, a horse, pigs, chickens.

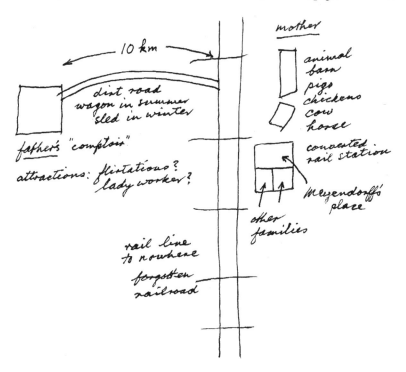

Layout of the homestead at Station Number 5.
Sketch by Alexandra (definitely not to scale).

Sofia took on the management of the homestead—feeding and caring for the animals, milking the cow, slaughtering poultry—tasks that she had previously been only vaguely aware of as the business of peasant women.

Meanwhile, apart from occasional absences, Vasily kept to his established routine at his *"comptoir,"* as they called his workplace.

Vasily and Sofia Meyendorff, with German Pointer pups.

Ten-year-old Alexandra was puzzled. What could her father be doing at work, now that the building of rail lines had ceased and trains were not running any more? Her mother and grandmother put her off with joking references to Vasily's reputation for gallantry, talking airily of "a lady friend, perhaps two ..." Only later, after the family made their escape by train to Estonia, did she realize that her father had indeed been working on an important railroad planning project.

The girls continued to read and study every day, but they found time to do the chores that fall to farm children everywhere. They also learned to care for and handle horses, and Alexandra became a good rider.

4

The Postcards Never Sent

Through Vasily and Sofia's sojourn at Station Number 5, civil strife continued to grow throughout Russia. With the complete collapse of the nation's currency and the ascendancy of the Bolsheviks in the major cities, Théophile and Hélène were no longer able to maintain their home in St Petersburg. Hélène and several members of her family moved to Estonia, where they divided their time between Tallinn and their summer vacation estate, Kumna. Hélène, then about sixty years old, also came to live from time to time at Station Number 5.

Hélène's robust good humor went far to boost the family's spirits there, and without planning to do so, she left a vivid account of their efforts to adapt to a life very different from the one they were used to.

For a long time Hélène had habitually communicated with distant friends and loved ones by postcards bearing spontaneous pastel sketches, each with a brief title or comment. At Station Number 5 she continued to put her thoughts on postcards, but in the chaos of the times the postal service was no longer operating reliably, so many of those postcards were never sent. Eventually a cache of them fell to Alexandra, and they are reproduced in the following pages. In the hundred years since Hélène dashed off these pastels, their colors have faded to various shades of mud, so little is lost in gray scale.

Hélène's inscriptions are shown in Alexandra's translation from Russian (upper case) and from French (italics).

SUNDAY REST

Vasily is taking Sunday off from his work at the office to be a *gentleman farmer*. In using the term "gentleman farmer" Hélène did not mean that Vasily's efforts on the farm were in any way those of a dilettante. Rather she alluded to his gentle manner with animals; it was a family joke that he used the Russian-language polite form of address when he spoke to cows and pigs.

IN FREEZING WEATHER WARM INSIDE

The wood-burning stove was good for heat as well as cooking.

Oh, these animals! We have to feed them, but what with? Sofia often found herself short of animal feed.

Father, bringer of food
Vasily is feeding a litter of German Pointer pups.

LET THE FAMILY HAVE EXERCISE
Trouble with balky animals.

ON MY WAY ... DISAPPOINTED
Maya is walking along the Railroad to Nowhere
toward a barter center where she hopes to
make a swap ... then returning, crestfallen,
with the same rooster.

QUICKLY,
OUTDOORS!
Alexandra
makes haste.

OKAY, COME
WITH ME
Maya finds that
pigs do not
understand
Russian.

Reading room
Maya (left) and Alexandra are engrossed in reading.

ON A SLED, THREE'S A CROWD
Vasily is ready to step off the sled in heavy going.

КЪ ОБЂДНЂ ПО ПЕРВОМ ПОРОШЂ

GOING TO CHURCH
DURING THE FIRST
SNOW
For Maya, it seems that
the snow is already too
deep.

GRANDFATHER'S GREAT-
COAT RECYCLED

Maya on the Railroad to
Nowhere, clad in one of
Grandfather Théodore's
military greatcoats cut
down to her size.

MAKING PLANS AT DAYBREAK
Alexandra and Maya receive their assignments.

A MORNING VISIT TO MISTER GOLINISHCHEV
The Russian flush toilet—"Mr Golinishchev" after
its inventor—is located higher up for a better flush.

*Venus emerging
from the waters*
Hélène portrays a
child as a miniature
classical Venus such as
might have adorned the
Meyendorff's home in
St Petersburg, and a
three-legged bath as
her point of emergence.
Note the stove (for
warmth) at right rear.

THE LATEST FASHION

Another of Hélène's
whimsical comparisons
of the family's country
lifestyle with that of
their life in St
Petersburg.

PREPARING THE "RUSSIAN STOVE" FOR BAKING
Wood-burning stoves of essentially the same design, with the fuel door at one side, oven door at front, were used throughout Russia in households both grand and humble.

GUESTS FOR TEA /
A. K. KANSHIN /
F. F. ROMANOVSKY

The girls help prepare for a visit from the guests named, their father's immediate superiors in the National Railroad hierarchy. The mismatched cups and saucers is another of Hélène's references to the family's reduced circumstances.

USING A SEIVE

Maya and Alexandra
are sieving grain to
make bread.

TODAY IS THE DAY FOR LEPESHKI

Lepeshki is a traditional
unleavened bread.

GOOD GIRLS

Alexandra (left) and Maya doing
homework. Maya is getting used to new
reading glasses.

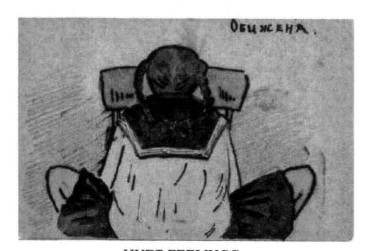

HURT FEELINGS

Even Alexandra, an amiable child,
could be touchy at times.

5

Estonia

In 1919, the fourth year of the Meyendorff's sojourn on the Railroad to Nowhere, the Russian Revolution attained its full fury. The institutions of civil society broke down completely. The Bolsheviks opened the jails and indiscriminately released all the prisoners. Desperate starving people wandered the countryside, and reports of pillage and murder by roving bands of brigands became commonplace. Few people—and no one with an aristocratic background—could feel safe anywhere in Russia. Many aristocrats with the necessary means and connections had already fled, many of them to the nearby states Estonia and Latvia. Some, including Alexandra's "Aunt Lily" Sheremetiev, had moved to Paris. Vasily and Sofia reluctantly decided it was time to put into effect their own, long-nurtured plan to find refuge on their Estonian family estate, Kumna.

In Estonia fighting was still going on between Bolsheviks and Estonian patriots, but the country remained calm compared with the turmoil in Russia.

Two years earlier, and just before its ouster by the Bolsheviks in 1917, the Russian Provisional Government had granted autonomy to Estonia, and the newly empowered Estonian government soon enacted reforms that led to a period of prosperity and social progress.

On Kumna, the result of these reforms was that the peasants and other workers on the estate became owners of the land they were working, and their cottages. However, Hélène retained title to the main house, as did "Uncle Golitsin" to his chalet. Vasily subsequently bought the chalet, and "Golitsinka" (Golitsin's House) became Vasily and Sofia's new home.

Vasily's escape plan tapped his connections in the Russian railroad system, disorganized now but still operating. He arranged to have two freight cars hauled by steam locomotive from Rybinsk to Station Number 5—by this time a modestly thriving farm—on the Railroad to Nowhere. Then with the family on board with all their possessions, including horses, cows, pigs, chickens and dogs, the train puffed back to Rybinsk, thence to Keila and Tallinn.

On Kumna the family lived a new life, very different from that of their summer vacations of the past. As year-round residents working a small plot of land on the estate formerly owned by them, their social status was now on a par with that of the local people. It was natural for them to have closer contact with communal activities and a traditional rural way of life.

To Alexandra this was all new and interesting. She found most interesting of all the preparation of sauerkraut, fermented cabbage, and its preservation for sustenance through the winter. Sauerkraut provided several essential nutrients—notably vitamin C—not otherwise available in the traditional winter diet, so the health of the community depended on keeping a good supply on hand until fresh vegetables came on in spring.

The methods used to preserve sauerkraut differed in detail, but they all used a pit—a sizable hole in the ground—as a refrigerator. One method started with a pit like a big shallow well lined with timber retaining walls. The pit was located in permeable soil, so that little water collected in it, and it was used year after year by the same group of families. At the end of the garden growing season and the approach of cold weather, the people came with vats of fermenting cabbage and lowered them into the pit. When the pit was full up to the frost line, they covered everything with hay up to ground level. After that, every week or so during the winter they lifted the hay and removed a portion of sauerkraut, perfectly preserved.

At the time they arrived in Estonia, neither Alexandra nor Maya had ever attended school. While they were not backward in their studies—they'd had lessons at home and were avid readers— they were held back by their lack of German. Their native Russian was spoken in parts of Estonia, but German, Estonian and Hungarian were the main languages, and only German was used in the schools. To overcome this difficulty, the Meyendorffs hired a tutor to give the girls a crash course in German, then had them placed in school in the lowest grade so that they could become fluent while they caught up with their age group.

At first, twelve-year-old Alexandra was embarrassed to find herself in a class with children half her age. But along with fluency in German, she developed a feeling of empathy for small children, and this was a feeling she retained long after being promoted to the grade of her age group.

After spending a year or two at Kumna and having established a farm on the estate, the family divided their time between the estate and the capital Kallinn, and Alexandra entered the equivalent of a high school there.

In summer, they came to Kumna and reverted to the leisurely ways of the past. Hélène with some of her children and grandchildren in the main house, and Vasily and Sofia and the girls in the chalet Golitsinka. Those were halcyon times when the upheaval in Russia, by this time reaching its climax, could be put out of mind for a while.

It was on one long day of summer that Alexandra felt the first pangs of adolescent longing. Always conscientious, she had a habit of doing summer homework on the second-floor balcony that went all the way around the chalet. She stayed with her study routine, but now chose a place on the balcony that would afford her an occasional glimpse of the handsome young man who lived in one of the cottages nearby. Sad to relate, the dull fellow never gave the slightest sign of noticing her.

Alexandra graduated from high school in 1924, when she was 17. The academic standards in Estonian schools were relatively advanced, so that completing high school was worth one to two years in an American college.

Those early years in Estonia were happy ones for Alexandra and her family and the several members of her extended family who had fled the turmoil in Russia. They all loved the quiet of Kumna, and even when they lived in the capital, a town less than twice the size of Rybinsk, they were never far from open country. Horse sports were their main diversion. Alexandra polished her riding skills, and she learned the art of driving a troika—reins in two hands, outer fingers controlling the outer two horses, index fingers and thumbs controlling the central lead horse. In winter, she and her cousins loved to ski snow-covered fields, hauled by a horse with Vasily in the saddle.

Fun on snow, Estonia 1922

Yes, those were happy years. But it was happiness that rang ominously hollow as the Bolsheviks tightened their grip on Russia and began to look outwards to their small-nation neighbors.

6

England

In 1928 Alexandra's parents thought the time was right for her to experience another culture—that of England. She didn't want to leave home, but Vasily and Sofia were adamant. They packed her off to stay for two years in the home of an aunt in a small town, Welwyn Garden City near London.

This "English aunt" was actually a more distant relation than "aunt" might suggest. She was Russian rather than English, the daughter of a prince from Georgia in Southern Russia. She had made contact with her St Petersburg relatives while attending college in the capital. She was an eccentric lady, an apparent hypochondriac given to making all sorts of unreasonable demands and projecting from her sickbed the power to see that her wishes were carried out.

Her husband was no more engaging. A professor at the London School of Economics and a man of scholarly distinction deeply involved in his work, he rarely spoke or laughed, and he paid no attention to Alexandra beyond the minimal requirements of etiquette.

Feeling like an intruder in this glacial household, Alexandra suffered the pangs of homesickness. Especially at first, she longed for the warmth of her family and the freedom and good cheer of life in Estonia.

Alexandra's time in Welwyn Garden City had a bright spot when her aunt introduced her to other distant relatives, a girl and two young men close to her own age. With them she sampled the pleasures of London—riding the tube and the tops of the red buses, Hyde Park, the theaters of Shaftesbury Avenue, the art galleries. But the joy was short lived; her imperious aunt saw to that.

Of all her aunt's demands, the most painful to Alexandra was that she sing in a choir. "An essential part of English culture," proclaimed the lady. Alexandra had never sung, had no idea how to sing and did not dare try. Fakery—hiding behind the music or lip-synching—went against her nature. Nor was it easy to bring off, since the choir mistress, a paragon of petty virtues, always made her stand in the front row.

To Alexandra, the choir members seemed a glum and dowdy group, unwilling to accept outsiders. But there was an exception, a pleasant and lively young woman with a good voice, the mainstay of the choir's sopranos. And this person was also shunned.

She and Alexandra became friends. They exchanged confidences in a neighborhood tea parlor, and eventually in the other's cozy, well-appointed flat. Little by little Alexandra learned about her new friend's life.

It involved a number of charming, wealthy gentlemen acquaintances, every one of them notable for their amusing—and, it seemed to Alexandra, bizarre—desires and interests. When she eventually tumbled to the realization that her friend's interest in these gentlemen was of a commercial nature, she was flabbergasted—she had never dreamed of such a thing! She maintained the friendship, but with redoubled care that her aunt did not find out about it.

* * *

Alexandra's stay in Welwyn City Gardens came to an end with the arrival, from America, of the Bradley family—a young Amherst College faculty member on a sabbatical at the London School of Economics, and his wife and four young children. The Americans, with their cheerful, polite manners, lit up the scene like a warm ray of sunshine. They needed part time help to look after the children, and Alexandra took the job eagerly.

Six months later, Professor Bradley took up a temporary diplomatic position in Geneva, and Alexandra went with the family and lived with them in a capacity that was part nanny, part governess. This worked out well, and soon it was settled that Alexandra would accompany the Bradley family on their return to America, and live with them in their home in Amherst, Massachusetts.

* * *

Her family in Estonia had never been far from Alexandra's thoughts, and soon she would be so far away from them! Of course she would have to see them one last time before leaving for America. She made the trip from Geneva, and the reunion was happy. But now that she had a wider experience of life, and dazzling expectations of her future in America, her family's affairs seemed modest in comparison. Indeed, only one detail of that last visit stayed in her mind—the Estonian ship on which she crossed the Baltic put on a splendid smorgasbord.

7

America

Alexandra at age 23 had no clear idea what she wanted to do with her life. It would be natural to suppose that from her experiences living with the Bradley family, and going back as far as her early schooling in Estonia, she wanted to make a career of work with children. But if that was her plan, it was an unconscious one. Consciously, she drifted from one thing to another as the fancy took her, without any plan at all.

It was Professor Bradley who set her on course for her life's work. He and Mrs Bradley introduced her to other Amherst faculty families and students, and through these contacts Alexandra quickly perfected her English and adapted herself to American customs. Subsequently Professor Bradley helped her get an exchange-student Visa for study in America, and a scholarship to Smith College in Northampton, Massachusetts.

So in 1931 Alexandra entered Smith College in an education program. In recognition of the superior standard of her high-school education in Estonia she was permitted to begin her tertiary education as a junior. She enjoyed her studies at Smith, and despite being a few years older than her classmates, she enjoyed the camaraderie of living in a dormitory. In 1933 she completed a Bachelor's degree in Education. Soon after that she completed a Master's as well, which the College awarded on the basis of a thesis alone. She left Smith with a clear purpose—a career in teaching in the United States public school system.

Alexandra Meyendorff at 26.
(Smith College year book, 1933.)

Though well prepared academically for public-school teaching, Alexandra still needed one other qualification: a permanent-residence visa, the forerunner of what is now called a "green card." To comply with the immigration authorities' rule that visas could be given only to people entering the country from abroad, Alexandra took a trip to Nova Scotia, and reentered in Maine. This seemingly pointless travel was not a burden—far from it. Eager for new experiences, Alexandra reveled in its kaleidoscope of novel vistas. And of course she was aware that, for thousands of people in Europe and Russia, the United States was a haven from Nazi and Soviet oppression, and for them a visa, and ultimately US citizenship could mean the difference between life and death. From the day of her naturalization as a United States citizen, her gratitude and affection for America never wavered.

* * *

Through her time at Smith College, Alexandra clung to her ambition to teach in the public school system. However, in the world-wide depression of the 1930s, despite her excellent credentials, she was obliged to go to work in a private school instead. She could have found a place nearby in New England, but because it promised travel and new experiences in different part of the country, she chose Virginia. The school was a private girls' school with a French theme, the "Ecole Française" in rural Virginia near Washington DC. Catering to some forty girls, all from wealthy families, it consisted of several handsome buildings set in surpassingly beautiful grounds. Alexandra's job was to teach French.

On her first visit to the school Alexandra noticed that the head mistress seemed more interested in the grounds and gardens than in her students, and she soon realized that this superficial attitude extended to education as well. Never mind teaching the girls to read Balzac or carry on a conversation in French; the aim of the Ecole Française was to give them a veneer of French culture just thick enough to impress their parents.

Instead of learning, the girls had to submit to discipline like that of a penitentiary. They had to wear a uniform of a sickening mauve color, and for even the briefest excursion outdoors they had to put on a mauve *pèlerine*, a cape of a style long outdated.

Most disturbing to Alexandra was a Friday assembly period in which the head mistress went over, one by one, the girls' shortcomings, infractions of rules, and so on, during the week.

The whole system went against Alexandra's idea of what teaching and learning should be; hard work, yes, but also joyful celebration in expanding the mind. There was no joy at the Ecole Française, and for the unfortunate girls any expansion of the mind had to wait until graduation.

Alexandra's happiest recollections of this period were of her Mondays off work. Free for a short time from the poisonous atmosphere of the school, she sauntered about museums and libraries in Washington, DC, and occasionally attended music performances. In art and music, she found freedom from banality.

* * *

After four years at the Ecole Française, Alexandra needed something completely different, and she found it in employment as a governess—a real governess now—for the ten-year-old daughter of the Dubonnet family. As she soon found out, however, she had entered another mean-spirited situation, but this time it was mean-spirited in a relatively entertaining way.

Monsieur Dubonnet was the heir to the fortune resulting from the success of the apéritif bearing his family name, and in 1939, along with his wife and daughter he had fled France just in advance of the Nazi invasion. His plan—or rather his wife's plan, for Mme

Dubonnet was the force behind all family decisions—was to wait out the war, in safety and comfort, in New York.

There was one catch—the Dubonnet fortune was frozen in a Paris bank, and the heir to it had arrived in America comparatively penniless. He was a plump, retiring little man accustomed to an easy life, and his reaction to finding himself broke in New York was one of vague bewilderment.

His wife, however, was more than equal to this parlous situation. For a start she was not French at all, but an American from Kansas, well used to living by her wits, and particularly to playing on her compatriots' susceptibility to the supposed mystique of French manners. A brazen spendthrift with a record of financially advantageous marriages and other liaisons with a succession of affluent gentlemen in America and Europe, she had good looks, a quick mind and a superficially pleasant personality—attributes perfectly fitted to cashing in on the credit of the Dubonnet millions. And cash in she did, most audaciously by persuading the management of the Savoy-Plaza that it would be to their ultimate advantage to allow the family the use of an entire floor of the hotel for the duration of the war.

So Alexandra became a member of the Dubonnet household at the Savoy-Plaza.

She quickly established a rapport with the child, but otherwise her situation proved difficult. The ten-year-old was devoted to her father, and in his vague way he may have returned the child's affection. But he made little effort to seek her out, and she often seemed too sad and anxious to attend to her lessons.

But Mme Dubonnet was Alexandra's main burden. The lady from Kansas was perennially short of money, forever hatching shady schemes to get by in the style to which she was accustomed. And Alexandra served, unwilling but inevitably, as her accomplice.

Madame Dubonnet's longest-running expedient was the card party. She lured ladies with names familiar in the society columns to high-stakes bridge games, where she contrived to win regularly. Perhaps she won with her guests' complicity. Or perhaps not; an excellent cards player, fast and accurate, and with scant respect for the rules, she was perfectly capable of winning unassisted.

For these affairs it fell to Alexandra to purchase the refreshments, and this had to be done on a skimpy budget because the Dubonnet household was often down to its last pennies. Madame Dubonnet regularly reprimanded Alexandra for not driving a hard-enough bargain at the pastry shop.

With her social credentials and her flair for fashion, not to mention her imposing address, Mme Dubonnet quickly became a New York celebrity. Hardly a week passed without a photograph of her in the newspaper society columns, smiling brilliantly as she flaunted a dazzling new costume. The columns named the suppliers of her outfits, but never inquired how she paid for them—which is a pity, because in newsworthy fact she didn't pay for them at all. After wearing a dress, she simply tossed it to Alexandra and told her to take it back with some excuse—"too short," or "didn't like that horrid shade of puce." Ritzy stores made it their policy to outfit Mme Dubonnet on credit—she compensated them in the coin of publicity, after all—but for Alexandra returning the goods they had nothing but contemptuous frowns.

In addition to these difficulties, Alexandra often had to beg to be paid her agreed-upon salary. When begging didn't work she packed her bags and threatened to leave, which she hated to do out of concern for the lonely Dubonnet child. On several such occasions Mme Dubonnet somehow scraped together the necessary cash, but in the end, having exhausted her bag of low-down tricks, she resorted to force.

Alexandra, in the course of her bag-packing routine, had just stepped inside one of the hotel's walk-in closets when Mme Dubonnet slammed the door shut and turned the key. But it didn't work; Alexandra happened to know that a duplicate key was to be found inside the closet in case of just such a situation, so she had no trouble escaping. And this time she left for good.

* * *

After leaving the employ of Mme Dubonnet, Alexandra returned to teaching. For a while she taught at another private school only slightly less depressing than the Ecole Française, and then at last she fulfilled her dream of teaching at a public school, this one in Bronxville, New York. She continued to teach there for two years, until the end of the war in Europe in 1945.

Throughout this period Alexandra was consumed with worry about the fate of her family. She had lost touch with them soon after the war broke out. Later she heard that her parents and her sister had been dragged to Poland. She resolved to go in search of them.

This was a daunting prospect. To go to Poland she had first to find a way to go to war-devastated Europe, still completely off-limits to all Americans except military personnel.

To make this first step, she joined the US Army and secured a posting in an Intelligence Unit in Frankfurt in Southern Germany, a city that had been largely reduced to rubble by Allied bombing.

Along with dozens of other multilingual workers, her job was to read letters that had been intercepted in post offices throughout Germany, and to report anything of interest to the US occupying forces.

That was as far as she got; she was refused permission to travel anywhere in Europe, let alone to a Soviet-occupied region. She never saw her family again, nor learned what happened to them.

APPENDIX

Historical Events	Date	Biographical Events
Russia: Serfdom has been abolished since 1861, but enormous social inequalities persist. The political system is increasingly strained as workers seek more freedom. Estonia: Through the 19th C the country has been ruled by Russia, while language, church and the legal system has been mainly German. With a resurgence of Estonian nationalism there is widespread agitation for freedom from Russian domination.	By 1900	Since the Middle Ages, branches of the Meyendorff (M) family have accumulated wealth and influence in Central and Eastern Europe, especially in Estonia and in Russia. Alexandra's grandfathers, brothers Théodore and Théophile M, between them own substantial properties in Ukraine, in the vicinity of Tallinn in Estonia and in St Petersburg (St P). Her maternal grandfather, Army General Théophile M, having served as an aide to the Tsar Alexander III until his death in 1894, continues as aide to his successor, Tsar Nicholas II.

Historical Events	Date	Biographical Events
Russia: workers organize, form soviets (workers' councils) press Tsar Nicholas II for reforms.	1900	
Estonia: Nationalistic uprisings are brutally repressed by the Russian authorities (1905).	1905	Vasily M, a railroad engineer, marries his cousin, Sofia M, in St Petersburg (St P). The couple make their home in St P in the house owned by Sofia's mother Hélène M.
Russia: Trans-Siberian railroad completed. Russo-Japanese War (1905). Russia suffers defeats by Japan. The Tsar accepts significant internal reforms. Estonia: Continued resurgence of nationalistic aspirations.	1905	Alexandra M (AM) is born in St P (1907). Her sister Maya is born in St P (1909).
Russia: the Tsar attempts to reverse reforms, thus inspiring increasing popular opposition to his rule. In both Russia and Estonia a tense social stability prevails in the years leading up to World War I (1910-1914).	1910	AM spends her early childhood in St P, enjoys family parties and excursions especially with grandmother Hélène. AM learns to read. She starts lessons in dancing, other skills needed for her anticipated debut in society.

Historical Events	Date	Biographical Events
Start of World War I (1914). German forces push eastward, invading Baltic states, Russia.	1914	Vasily is sent to the war zone to work on restoration of war damage to Russian railroads.
Russia: Army suffers defeats to Germany. Food shortages and economic collapse follow throughout the country.	1915	Vasily is reassigned to Sochi (Caucasus). Sofia and the two children follow to Sochi. The family moves to Rybinsk.
Russia: War effort flounders. Economic collapse is complete.	1916	With a Swiss governess, AM learns to speak French, and also to read a little. In lieu of pay, Vasily accepts a small parcel of railroad property (Station Number 5) near Rybinsk. AM frequents an abandoned library, "La Bibliotèque Rose," where she perfects her reading knowledge of French. The family takes up farming at Station Number 5.

Historical Events	Date	Biographical Events
Russian Revolution, part 1: The Tsar abdicates. A provisional government takes over (1917). Estonia: National autonomy is granted by the Russian provisional government (1917). An Estonian Elected Assembly is formed but it is forced underground by political extremists.	1917	Hélène joins the family at Station Number 5. Railway construction has come to a halt, but Vasily retains a responsible position in the national railroad system. The family flees by train to Estonia (1918), where they live on the rural estate, "Kumna," then entirely owned by the Meyendorffs. Later they divide their time between Kumna and Tallinn.
Russian Revolution, part 2: Radical Bolsheviks overthrow the provisional government, seize control of the major cities (1917). Civil strife spreads throughout the country. Bolsheviks murder Tsar Nicholas II and family (1918). End of World War I (1918). Russia: Civil War 1918-1921.	1917	AM(12) learns German with a tutor, attends an Estonian German-language elementary school starting in classes with much younger children.

Historical Events	Date	Biographical Events
Estonia: After withdrawal of German forces, fighting continues between Estonian troops and Bolshevik forces (1919). Estonia adopts sweeping property reforms. Estonia and the new Soviet Union sign a peace treaty (1920). Russia: The Bolsheviks gain control of the entire country (1923).	1920	AM attends an Estonian secondary school in Tallinn. She enjoys outdoor activities in the Estonian countryside, including horse riding and caring for horses. She completes secondary school with her age group.
Estonia: The country enjoys peace, independence, democratic government (1919-1939). USA: Stock Market crash (1929) marks the beginning of the Great Depression.	1925	Her parents send her to England to live with relatives near London. AM learns English, English customs. While in England she serves as nanny in the family of a visiting Amherst College faculty member, Professor Bradley.
	1925	AM visits her family in Tallinn. Still in the employ of the Bradley family, AM accompanies them on their return to their home in Amherst, Mass.

Historical Events	Date	Biographical Events
USA: Widespread unemployment persists through the Great Depression (1930-40). Start of World War II (1939).	1930	AM enters an education program at Smith College in Northampton, Mass. She graduates from Smith with bachelor and master degrees in Education (1934), becomes a US citizen, seeks a teaching position in a public school. Unable to find a public-school position, she teaches in a private girls' school (1934-39). She loses touch with her family in Estonia.
Estonia: Soviet occupation, installation of Stalinist socialist system. (1940). German invasion (1941). Estonia: Germans retreat. Soviets regain control despite resistance by Estonian guerrillas (1944-1946).	1940	AM takes a position of governess and factotum with the Dubonnet family at the Savoy-Plaza Hotel in New York City. She resigns her position with the Dubonnets and returns to teaching, finding at last a position in a public school (Bronxville NY).

Historical Events	Date	Biographical Events
End of World War II. Soviets occupy Eastern Europe including Poland and East Germany. Start of the Cold War between USA and Allies, Soviet Union.	1945	AM serves in a US Army Intelligence Unit in Frankfurt, Germany (1945-46). She strenuously seeks permission to travel in the Soviet Sector in search of news of her family, but is denied.

ACKNOWLEDGMENTS

I am grateful to all members of the Hunterdon County NJ Library Writers' Group who offered thoughtful comments on my writing, particularly Tony Athmejvar, Roy Brown, Marlene Cocchiola, Morgan Hansen, Jay Langley, Nawaz Merchant, Mark Snyder, Arlene Tkatch, and Evelyn Van Nuys. Special thanks to Mark Snyder for help in the preparation of the manuscript, to Ilya Mikhalev for nuanced comments on the captions of the postcards never sent, and to Matt Marchment for restoring a badly damaged portrait of Théodore Meyendorff.